Don Walls

# Inside Out

*For my friends*

First published in 2006 by
DEADGOOD Publications
England

Copyright © Don Walls 2006. All rights reserved. No part of this publication may be reproduced, stored in a retrieval system, or transmitted, in any form or by any means, without the prior permission of the author.

Cover illustration by Don Walls

Also by Don Walls:
"In the Shed", published in 2005 (ISBN 0-9546937-1-X)

Printed by Abbey Print, Hemingbrough, North Yorkshire, England

# CONTENTS

| | |
|---|---|
| Roses, wild thyme | 1 |
| Fishing for Pike with my Father | 2 |
| Cheltenham Crescent | 3 |
| Dog Lover | 4 |
| Tongue | 5 |
| Blitz | 6 |
| Recovery | 7 |
| Unmade Poem | 8 |
| Shoes | 9 |
| Recarpeting the Universe | 10 |
| Our War | 11 |
| Us Feet | 12 |
| Points in Time | 13 |
| My Singing Voice | 14 |
| Pet Pig | 15 |
| My Cat Skinny | 16 |
| My Bad Manners | 17 |
| I could die for a pee | 18 |
| Mute Swans | 19 |
| We walked by the river my mother and I | 20 |
| Gardener | 21 |
| For Mary | 22 |
| Since the appropriate words | 23 |
| I lock my rage in the garden shed | 24 |
| Story | 25 |
| Barber's Shop | 26 |
| My Secret | 27 |
| Stones | 28 |
| My Embarrassments | 29 |
| For Sabahattin (A political prisoner) | 30 |
| For B | 31 |
| Night Out with Mary | 32-33 |
| My Mind is an Elephant | 34 |
| Three Letters to Flavius | 35-40 |
| On Pylons Shedding Intelligence, Knowledge | 41 |
| Senior Citizen | 42 |

## CONTENTS (continued)

| | |
|---|---|
| Beggar | 43 |
| Growing Old Gracefully | 44 |
| In Memory of Terry | 45 |
| Ken | 46 |
| Rabbit | 47 |
| Library | 48 |
| My Stubbornness | 49 |
| Pheidippides | 50-51 |
| Water splashes over the edge | 52 |
| For M | 53 |
| Junkie | 54 |
| For S | 55 |
| I'm always ahead of myself | 56 |
| for Mr L who talked about going back | 57 |
| Intruder | 58 |
| Do-it-All | 59 |
| Shearwaters off Istanbul | 60 |
| House | 61 |
| Aftermath | 62 |
| Joiner | 63 |
| Wagtails | 64 |
| The Lane | 65-67 |
| Stag | 68 |
| Arrest | 69-70 |
| The Years | 71 |
| Eyes | 72 |
| Whatever I love | 73 |
| Our Hens | 74 |
| Key | 75 |
| Onions | 76 |
| bookmite | 77 |
| My Mistakes | 78 |
| Potatoes | 79 |
| Dante - Addendum | 80-82 |
| Shed | 83 |

Roses, wild thyme
and all the flowers down the lane
buddleia, bay
and the call of ringdove in the lime,
but oh that she were here today
in wind and rain
and all the flowers some other time.

**Fishing for Pike with my Father**

Early morning. Mist lingering.
We prepared to fish the river my father and I
for the great pike, Lord of the Waters.
My father thought he'd seen him once,
his shadow drifting in and out of reeds.
The old folk talked of him: voracious, gorged on anything
- his own fry, lead weights, wives.
Solitary Lord of his Domain,
olive green - white spots mimicking light in water.
Immense, they say he could drag a mallard under.

My father cast the spinner
to glint and lure in the surface light.
Then reeled it in. Cast and reeled.
The plop and the ratcheting. Then silence,
and where mist touched the water, a wave
as if something had surfaced then slipped into the depths.
My father cast again. And again.
And suddenly the line was taut and the rod bent over
like the willows that lined the bank. And the long play began:
hours of it, reeling the line in - water springing off its tautness,
then the slackness and the diving back to the depths
and the tautness again
and my body swerving
first with my father and then the fish.
It was like bringing a huge mystery to the surface
something that kept me wondering for years
in the depths of my childhood.
For a moment I thought the fish would heave my father in.
Then my father heaved him out.

Gills gasping, his whole body thrashed the ground boking barbs blood,

eyes glazed

I stared across the waters.

**Cheltenham Crescent**
(For Mary, suffering from Alzheimer's)

Her father so strong
he raised her on the palm of his hand,
her mother's ginger, chocolate cake
sumptuously clung
to the roof of her mouth,
the generous sun
red winters
and ferns of ice
on the path
glass,

so she wants to go home to Cheltenham Crescent
- skipping, hopscotch
croggying - swifts
twilight-starlings
shrill and settling
chips and gossip
Floss
riving the night
and the hug for the road
wet flags and snow
the din of sparrows in the eaves
make-believe
where the rage of the world found no way in
- blessed in the kitchen with words and bread,
sorrow just the darker side of stories
her mother read.

**Dog Lover**

I keep an imaginary dog in my head
- my wife won't have one in the house -
and I teach him to sit
and fetch a stick
and all the tricks
roll and beg,
and now and again he needs to pee
so I keep an imaginary lamp post, tree,

then I give him his head
and he romps in the grass
sniffs dog and bitch
mounts whichever
- which end is which -
trial and error

and rapt I stare
and my wife suspects a dog in my head
and locks me in the garden shed.

**Tongue**

Troglodite
licks lollies
stamps

ancient,
no eyes, feet.
Tuts, tastes
swallows, spits.

Explores the teeth
anything alien obsessing it.

Archetype:
- bell clapper,
shoe flap.

Daft,
touches the nose, flutes.

**Blitz**
(For Marie and Doug)

Beneath the stairs
a flask of cold tea, gas masks.
The blast
and my sister combed and combed her hair.
The smell of gas
cracks
ash,
the judder, the thud
then silence
sudden and suspect
as if destruction might come back.
I picked my scab.
The police - a bomb in the street
I grabbed the cat,
my comics in a carrier bag,
chestnuts, ammonites.
My father's tic, roofs burning
and what I'd never seen before
nimbus glowing orange-red,
Pickering Terrace no longer there
- gone the high wall we climbed for a dare
and I thought of those I saw each day
on my way to school,
the heat seared my face yards away.

**Recovery**
(For Emily and Ben)

Blur.
A spasm of will
holds back vomiting
and thoughts swoop in
peck at my mind.
I shoo them away.
The sun's a menace.
The ceiling arid.
Blue nurses hovering.

Pee.
Pills, drip.
Whatever it is
I'm harnessed to,
I wait on the edge
of what happens next,
pillows rumpled
- a world of curtains, patterns
terrain of the walls
the coldness of ice
and thoughts swoop back
swift as swifts - this way, that:
road tax
rain
- my tiles on the roof
and what I said or should have said.
What if?

I know the counterpane inside out.
Outside the frost.
It's never been so white before.
What a miracle my hand is
in sheets, shadows
- legs, toes.
Everthing close
and a closer light
round those I know.

**Unmade Poem**
(After Tracey Emin - Unmade Bed)

This is an unmade poem
its stanzas a mess
like clothes on my bed
words just left,
underpants, vests
folds of chance
as the landscape adapts to knees and toes
hills, dales,
and all the perceptions of where I am
in shifts of rhythm, rhyme
and meaning slipping like a quilt to the floor
pillows restive,
panic, sweat
the desultory straightening of the clothes
the endless tinkering with a line
- a word an image I may never find
the searching chatter in my mind.

**Shoes**

Needs nil survive.

Pragmatic,

negotiate cobbles, ice.

Never smile.

Talk to gravel.

Sit out dark years beneath the stairs.

Never complain.

Have nothing to hide.

No ambition.


Abandoned, remind us of someone else.

**Recarpeting the Universe**
(For Suzie and Jack)

Today I recarpet the Universe
wall to wall.
All I need is in the garden shed
- rolls of space and rolls of time
ruler, set square
tacks and glue,
Ptolemaic maps
almanacks,
so I know what's happening when and where
since space is littered with stars and stuff
frayed, threadbare
but first I practise on the bathroom floor
round the bath and round the loo
with carpet ends
- parallel thoughts of the room next door.
Then well wrapped up - brolly, Yorkshire cap
gaberdine mac
a flask of soup
and space-time rolls on a Tesco trolley
I launch myself on Clifton Ings.
My friends are there,
celebrities, the Lord Mayor
me mounting the air
- Land's End
Finistere,
heading for the Universe.

**Our War**

My parents sat by the wireless through the war.
Faces serene,
they listened to the King,

us kids, we fought the Germans on the Ings,
words bursting like handgrenades
shells screeching.
Some of us V.C.s.

On the wireless victories: El Alamain, Tobruk
dead countless
- my mother's face flushed,
my Father's embrace.

We strafed every terrace this side of town
held the footbridge
till the sun went down
and crossed the dunes on Clifton Green, meadows
of the Ings
mopping up, taking prisoners
hid and ambushed in willows, shadows.

The wireless crackled and spat
- howitzers, messerschmidts, bats.
Gas green as grass
tanks rumbling
blockades
- stones, bricks
and arms outstretched
we bombed the panzers, the S.S.,
stabbed the air and killed the Bosch,

and never growing old
some of us lay down in England's green pastures
then cycled north to the aerodrome
to see what the P.O.W.s looked like
before they left for home.

**Us Feet**
(For Jim and Pam Webster - chiropodists)

We've been stuck with him for seventy years or more
- in darkness learnt the daily routine:
a turning here, a stopping there.

At night sometimes he stares at us, our form primeval,
but mostly, of course, we're never noticed
(nobodies in the scheme of things)
unless there are reasons:
bunions, ingrowing nails, athlete's foot,
and so we scour our minds for anything enhancing the role of feet:
toes painted, designer sandals on the beach
and whatever empowers us:
massage and reflex,
or courses held in stately homes
on not neglecting the foot in sex.

**Points in Time**
(For Ruth and Steve)

There are many points in time,
some a change in direction
like the corner of a square,
acute like a triangle
- birth and death
and all the official events
of when and where,

then the moments that come flooding back
while walking your dog or brushing your teeth:
blankets of snow and you shaking the larch
and both of us white,
to-whit to-whooing
and the owls answering back
the storm at night
and us in the tent
and it rained and rained
and the rain came through and both of us drenched
and all we could do was lie there and laugh
and we laughed and laughed
and the rain didn't stop
and we couldn't stop laughing.

**My Singing Voice**
(For Emily)

I keep my singing voice in the garden shed.
Once it roamed free
and shredded silence late at night
boomed down pipes and shaking trees
it split the bricks and crumbled cement
shook foundations
and shudderd the safety of the house
and birds described an arc of distance
far from where they heard my voice.

Then of destruction and death the worst
my poor canary pampered for years
on quality millet and cuttlefish shells
was swept away in a blast of song,
scrunched on its back and legs in the air
- a ball of feathers small and precious
beneath a wing his little head.
I cried for days
then locked my voice in the garden shed.

**Pet Pig**

I keep a pet pig on the garden lawn
and we grunt together at trespassing cats.
I scratch his back
and stroke his snout
and read him stories:
three pigs and the wolf.
Fiction he loves - threats - cold sweat,
Miss Piggy in love.

He cringes at words like piggish and pigsick
pig's ear and poke
and connotations of the police
and once, the privet overgrown,
I honed my shears
- stone on steel -
you could hear him squeal across the Ings
and to calm him down I sang to him
and chucked his chin.

Down on all fours, snout in the trough,
I've learnt to scoff.
He's learnt to stand up
cover up
shifty, blush.

**My Cat Skinny**

Shot.
Sheenless.
I found him in the long rye grass
one eye shut, one eye open
and a glint of why
in the light of my torch.

My cat Skinny - black, sleek
leapt at anything
- leaves, flies.
Moth and mouse-cat
knobbles of spine
beneath my palm-cat.
On my lap
belly, chest,
on my neck.
How close could he get-cat?

**My Bad Manners**

My wife tracks them down
in the kitchen on the stair
wherever I am they're always there
round my feet in my speech
language bristling on the street
the way I eat gluttonous cram
slam the door
slurp and burp,
wherever they are she flushes them out
sharpens her glance and puckers her mouth
squints and scowls
at night she drums my ears in bed
so I lock them in the garden shed.

I could die for a pee
and pull up by the wood.
Darkness, the bastard, has swallowed the hills.
The rain unforgiving
I've no idea where I am.
The nettles, the wankers, let me know,
brambles grasping.
There's an owl hanging on.
Light rims the hills.
Eternity, the swine, has it all his own way
or thinks he has!
- time stops in the rain
in my endless sluicing of the grass.

**Mute Swans**
(For Rachel and James)

Two swans - cob and pen
on the river's drift.
Whiteness of necks in olive green waters

- conduits of light surfacing.
Beaks dripping, glistening...

Andante in reeds.
The mind's drift:
snow untouched,
white lilies in rain.

Stillness, mist

and two swans thwacking the air.
The sound of whiteness winging upstream.

We walked by the river my mother and I
- a swan going nowhere on still waters
and the strangest feeling that nothing mattered,
ripples finding the water's edge.
Yo-yo of midges,
mists of silence.

Then suddenly out of the dark Spring, swifts
shrill and swooping
as if I'd never seen them before
and me flying with them
- curves, ellipses
and everywhere blueness.
My mother's hand on my shoulder.

**Gardener**
(For my father)

Sleet, drizzle
beds of snow shifting
wetness
the first spider stringing thread
frozen light
woodlice.
Greenness. Greenfly,
and where had they been all winter, he asked me,
as if there was something I was keeping back.
Sounds bare to the sky: dog-fox, owl
and we fired the nettles at the garden's end
the dense smoke-fog covering the sunflowers.
For days my clothes stank of greenness burning.
And there were mice sometimes on the edge of sight
and once a weasel
and he'd tell me in nudges where to look.
Fledglings strident in the hedge -
their long throats.
And once we dug up bones
and placed them together and built a fox
and I saw it bound away
- a deep red dog-fox
in the length of the day
and he lifted me up to the water butt

- looking down at him looking up at me,
the long sun shifting.

**For Mary**

A few glimpses still:
snow, the Alps
dazzling in Tuscany
wine in Graz
the Guggenheim, Bilbao,
surprise-remembering
red roses in France,

and a childhood ago
clear as this photograph
- school-girl gawky
stains round your mouth -
surprised by deer this far south
- a mouse in the grass
sparrowhawk, owl,

and now the lessening of light
and the blurring of borders - morning, night
and you setting out
and the police bring you back
and both of us lost,

frost
where fireweed grew
the logic of blackthorn
white as snow
before the leaves peep through.

Since the appropriate words
didn't appear in the appropriate column,
I suppose you think I'd forgotten.
Well, I had!
You know me, no head for dates.

I bet you're upset in one of your moods like you used to be,
with a bit of shouting and then regret,
but just because memory's shed
what happened when,
don't think it's dead
it has its own ways,
or why did I write this poem then?

I lock my rage in the garden shed.
You can hear him at night
banging the door and swearing through cracks.

The neighbours have had enough of him.
Binmen, postmen.
I could, of course, abandon him
dump him at Scarborough, Flamborough Head
but like the proverbial cat
he would find his way back
- on the doorstep in the morning.

I never know what makes him rave
behave outrageous
the English language torn to shreds
in torrents of words:
wankers, dickheads

but just in case it's this or that
I only walk him late at night
after folk have gone to bed.
Then lock him back in the garden shed.

**Story**

It's about wherever I am.
The mood of this room in the evening light.
The ghost of our dog unravelling scents,
and it's like reading a book from the middle, the end
or skipping a chapter and filling in spaces.
It's about this crack on the path,
a canyon for creatures beyond the eye,
or the sea and its imagery of depth and shingle.
It's about moss and wild thyme,
stars awakening and the immensity of chance
and moments passing into the passing of things -
the archaeology of love,
and how a few words might burst into bud.
It's about the absence of things - shoes by the door
and how something small like a finch's egg is a reminder.
It's about how desire never goes away,
of being somewhere else in someone else's mystery.

**Barber's Shop**
(For David Holland)

Kneeling on the chair. Twin room in the mirror.
Queues after school. Tom Smythe coming in,
bike clips still on,
'Shift starts at five...'
and 'young Don won't mind.'
I'd politely say 'no' and think, 'bloody hell.'
Shabby magazines.
Short back and sides - pre-arranged by Dad.
Ted's chatter and clipping,
'Tell yer mam to back Dante in the three o'clock.'
How many years before daring a question:
'D'yer think York'll win Satday,
Jones out through injury?'
or something I'd glanced at
in the '*Sporting Pink*.'
Then a head round the door,
'Durex please,
overnight pack of twenty-four,'
and I'd smile with the rest,
Ted wetting his brush
- 'Er I'd rather have Brylcreem,'
and Ted stepping back
with his large hand mirror
as I glimpse myself
through mirrors and mirrors.

**My Secret**

I keep my secret in the garden shed.
By secrecy I foster it,
glance over my shoulder as I fetch it out on a moonless night
pretending not to see my wife, watching with the lights turned off.
I walk it on the Ings and round the block.

And word gets round I keep a secret in the garden shed.
Outside swarms of kids
neighbours, folk from streets away.
Reporters from *The Mirror* and *The Sun*.

And all this makes my secret huge
everyone asking 'How does it fit in the garden shed?'
In fact, I keep it in a box
with all the paraphernalia of nails and screws and next year's seeds
and should it get out and run between their legs
no one would see it
- all eyes focused on the garden shed.

**Stones**

bivouacked
hordes from Asia

sing shanties in a gravelly voice

bloom on beaches reds and blues

calligraphers in frost
commune with moss

you never know which way they face
or if they sleep

**My Embarrassments**

My embarrassments chase me round the lawn
and round the block.
Desperate sometimes I just drive off
but they're in the boot
on the back seat
even in the driving seat.
They're on the Ings,
in the cold and in the heat,
in the park.
They stand in groups around my bed
remind me what I've done and said,
luminous in the sleepless dark.

**For Sabahattin** (A political prisoner)

I

Midnight.
A knocking on the door.
Knocking. KNOCKING.

Knick knacks scurried.
Chairs like gazelles.
Cushions screamed
and muffled their ears.
Mirrors froze.

II

The pleasure of going there, just turning up,
was the generous opening of the door
- the welcome-in as wide as smiles
with a score of questions like
*'Where have you been?'*
*'Why didn't you write?'*
*'We were only talking about you tonight.'*
And all this with a kiss on both cheeks
before I went in.
I wish there were more doors like his.

**For B**

'Ashes to ashes, dust to dust' -
the coffin was down in the grave
and we around it looking in

when I heard the snort of horses
the thud of their hoofs on the turf,
and I knew he'd have watched the horses,
so I turned and watched the horses
till they came and nuzzled my hands.

**Night Out with Mary**

I

9.00pm - a frog the size of Brimham Rocks
sat in the middle of Lendal Bridge
and we stopped and watched, Mary and I.
We'd never seen a frog that size:
you could see the power that hinged its legs.

Then kids arrived and one of them poked it with a stick
and unleashed a leap
that shuddered the bridge on Richter ten.

The amphibian temporarily eclipsed the moon.
Where would it land,?
Manchester, Leeds, Scarborough sands?

Mary smiled.

We leapt like kids up Station Hill.

II

3.00am
Two dragons frolicked near Bootham Bar.
Both spouted fire.
One cocked its leg and the road was awash,
but we went across, Mary and I
and they both smouldered down,
though their tongues were hot.
Mine raised its chin,
I tickled its neck
and Mary fed hers an egg and cress sandwich left over from lunch.

They rumbled and rolled
plumes of flame lit up the walls.
Then the police arrived

and the dragons awed,
spaniel-sad they licked our hands.
Firemen led them both away.

We hung around the bar a bit, Mary and I.
I gently stroked her tilted chin.
She held a sandwich to my mouth.

III

5.00am
We turned down the Shambles, Mary and I,
where a mammoth was stuck
between Pickerings and the craft shop on the other side.

Mary offered it her liquorice stick
but you could tell by its eyes the mammoth was scared,
so we pulled its trunk and shoved its rump.
poured olive oil down either side,
but the beast didn't budge.

'I've got an idea', Mary said,
'visualise it floats away.'
(Mary was into things like that).

So, I closed my eyes
and in the tide of morning light
I imagined the mammoth float away.

Mary's magic, I smiled to myself

- then peeped at where the mammoth was stuck
between Pickerings and the craft shop on the other side.
There was nothing there, save Mary, of course,
who smugly licked her liquorice stick.

**My Mind is an Elephant**

Sometimes I pretend to be an elephant.
I do this in the bedroom and trumpet.
My wife has heard it all before.

I just fit in. I dare not lean,
the bed would collapse
the walls would crack,
the floorboards creak.

From the street neighbours, kids
wave and cheer.
In fact, I feel enormously important
and swing my trunk and flap my ears,
but it never lasts.

On the stairs I hear my wife,
her visceral rumblings,
and glimpse myself in the bedroom mirror,
shrinking fast.

**Three Letters to Flavius**

Letter 1

Dear Flavius,
I'm writing this in the light of my oil lamp.
In the hills the wolves are howling.
At night all sounds threaten: owl, last year's leaves.
Between the trees the darkness is tangible.
I smell the wood smoke from enemy camps.

In Rome we talked of glory.
Here, all that matters the will to survive.
Men fevered, festering
driven by fear, rage sometimes.
I no longer know what bravery means.

Tonight the army gathers round the shrine of Mithras.
Tomorrow the attack - the smashing of skulls, the slicing of legs,
slow dying and barbarians crucified.
Bogged in valleys mind-sick men.
The generals make a ceremony of them
- cowards at the point of spears, driven over the precipice.
So many corpses, the rats grow fat.

At moments like these, Flavius, I remember that summer
- your villa in the hills - fireflies beneath the olive trees
and Portia singing and playing the cithara,
your sons practising the broadswords.

Here, in the army unease:
a whispering of corruption in Rome
- arms and fortunes
and men say things on campaign, Flavius,
which will never reach the history books.

Recently, my melancholia's darkened my thoughts again.
I used to visit a Greek doctor in Rome
who treated my spirit with gentle talk and valerian.

Now, at least, the snows are receding
and the first Spring flowers peep from crannied rocks
- snowdrops and celandines.
At night we drink mead
- last night with Septimus.
Wounded, today he leaves for Rome.
I hear the city's full of quacks.

Do you ever see Philippa, Flavius?
- her father, a doctor of high repute, treated me for the fever.
I've heard she sat for the artist Plotinus.

Here, rain, rain ...
The generals push two legions forward
- mud the enemy - supplies immobile, slopes unclimbable.
You know the scenario, Flavius.
Some fool, new blood from Rome, had a testudo dragged to the front.

Rome.
In Rome the war's a war on maps.
Here the campaign has reached an impasse
and we're treated to acrobats, women from Rome
and barbarians pitted against each other
while the commanders sit like prefects in the public arena
dreaming of villas on the banks of the Tiber
and round them the sycophants.
The slaughter spreads. Strategic defeats.
Vultures. Crows.

This morning over the hills a glint of sun,
geese
and I thought I glimpsed a swallow, Flavius.
My longing for Spring, perhaps.

A young lad, a farmer from Caria, brought in a rabbit skinned
and shared it between ten men or more
while in the tents of gold, oysters from Ostia
brought by mule train in boxes of ice over the Alps.
Rank fills bellies, Flavius. Hunger's a wound.
Fevers decimate the men
and the surgeon is overworked. Tents groan with the wounded
- you can hear them all night with the owl and the nightjar.

The army is fading, Flavius.
The army is fading
no matter how much generals and senators talk of the glory of Rome
no matter how many bulls are sacrificed for victory skirmishes.
Tell me Flavius, what has changed since the first Caesars?

Letter 2

Last week, Flavius, I spent with the moor tribes.
Late March - drizzle, mists - light draining from the valleys.
The little ceremony of the cup and the ring:
spring water offered to the elders.
Then the huddling.
Wheezing smoke and reek of fear.
Leaf-sound. Wolf-howl.
Wings to beat the earth away
and every night the black cough.
The old woman with juices - heather herbs
and Death on his nightly rounds.

An old man sings the ice song to ward off cold, to ward off evil.
There's a little animal here, Flavius, lives only a year
- a tremulous alertness wears it out.
All night wind sounds out rocks.

Dawn and up with the hunters.
Hoar frost. Heather glow.
Then the stag dance - antler hands above their heads.
Rabbit dance, rabbit ears - magic for their hunting,
and Athuen leads us across the moors.
An intelligence like his we've never seen in Rome, Flavius,
reads shadows, rocks and senses wolves a league away.

We drive a stag into the moor bog.
Suck and drag of tired legs. Eyes frantic for flight.
Swift spears bring it down.
Meanwhile, over the ridge, their own village raided
by the Outlanders from the Black Hills
and their women folk and children hide in the valley of reeds.
Overhead the searching wind.

The skirmishes never end, Flavius
and no one remembers a time of peace.
Every night a sortie and the weaving of little twig dolls
for each warrior to give him strength,
touched and blessed by the Shaman elder.
Then the spear dance, the dagger song
and the apotheosis of the tribe
and the warriors setting out into the darkness.

Daybreak and the fearful coming back
- speared and bleeding,
and the old woman with leaves and sutures of grass
and the warriors who didn't come back
and the weaving of their replicas in long moor grass,
buried on the high moors in a plenitude of stones
and the tribe willing them to cross into the darkness.
And then the birth in the bleakness.
The chant of voices willing the child into light
and the Shaman pronouncing a blessing
- a warrior child for the glory of the tribe.
I recognized the word glory, Flavius,
- it's in our Latin - Gloria.
So abstract I never knew what it meant.

Letter 3

Dear Flavius,
Chlorus died last week and lies in the Mithraeum.
The legions of the north file past his catafalque,
but even before the ring of funeral orations fades into history,
men's eyes tell the story of unease.
You've seen it all before Flavius,
the not knowing where power sits,
a tremor running through the army
- mumblings and mistrust filtering down even to the ranks,
men fawning round centurions, generals.
A dagger in the dark.

This morning, Flavius, I've come to the hills.
There's a little spot just before the greenness of the vale merges into heather land,
and above there's a ridge dividing land from sky.

Clouds in legions come marching down,
black with silvery chinks
- high and cumulus in summer suns.
I've fallen asleep here in this greyness, Flavius,
awakening in a mist of light - tones shifting -
the trees greener, the freshness of the grass, the silver stream,
and the ridge, olive green across the sky.

From where I'm sitting there's a path leading up to the heatherland
(I hear the bee buzz in my head)
and beyond is the kingdom of the winds
- the homeland of Athuen and the tribes.
From rocky outcrops eyes recognise me leagues away.
On my arrival the tribe is seated beneath the boulders in ritual welcome
and offer me a little wooden goblet of ice-water,
flavoured with last season's berries
and they make gifts of beads like our melon beads
- which I'm sending for Portia and Philippa -
together with a horn for your Roman wine.

The women weave chains of early flowers for the season's fortune
and the elders invoke the favours of the gods
- the hill gods, the sky gods, the gods of the hunt,
and the tribe join in -
murmurs at first swelling to a crescendo,
and then the dance - wolf dance
and for the children the little mouse dance even.
And everyone kisses the elders' hands.
Here, any man can become an elder Flavius
as he grows in wisdom - the wisdom of the seasons, of nature.

Then they all assemble to wish me goodbye
and kiss my hands
and pour water over my sandals,
so my journey flows.

Athuen accompanies me to the Roman camp.
I enter the camp as the greyness and drizzle drifts in from the west.
The sun has been occluded for days.
The crows are pairing and caw from the parapets in dubious welcome.

Sentries eye me with suspicion
and everywhere a formal greeting - no warmth in words.
Once I believed in words and even made speeches,
but now keep silent like the rest.
A man has no voice in public office, Flavius.
It's all manoeuvring - shifts of allegiance
and the State itself is an Ocean
to be trawled for personal gain.
Octavius arrives tomorrow. General of the north.
They say he is of the opposing faction.
Rank, Flavius, is equated with intelligence
and no one gainsays one's superiors
- no sooner appointed than they're experts in everything.

Outside, the first crocuses peep through the fresh greenness
- soon a flood of yellow.
Tomorrow Caius and Antonius leave for Rome with the mule train.
Tonight in their honour we'll drink mead,
not the rich heady wine of Rome, but I like it.
It reminds me of the heather bees,
the moors and my friends the barbarians.

**On Pylons Shedding Intelligence, Knowledge**
(After Jean Sprackland - Jodrell Bank)

It began with the cows
staring knowingly as we crossed the fields
and there was something in the bleat of sheep
as if surprised how clever they were,
and in the orchards brilliant apples
the whiff of intelligence in the air
grass knowing everything,
shrewd weeds
and overhead waves of instant learning spilling spelling
mathematics,
and smart graffiti across the Dales
in bus shelters, stations:
the spiral helix, quantum mechanics,
and every weekend
clever picnics beneath the pylons
from Harrogate to Pen-y-Ghent.

**Senior Citizen**

Early morning everything irks:
the din of the birds,
bumping into, dropping things
- Newtonian Physics gets on my nerves.
Spring - ground elder overtakes
- the freezing sun, drizzle, flakes,
summer and then the kids are off
swarming, scoffing
leaves on the track
and then the eternal cycle's back:
January, February
the greyness, the gloom
the wife's relations down from Troon
unseating my belly,
telly - soaps
the Top of the Pops
mobile phones and internet
snow and then the traffic stops
odd socks - relationships
and nothing fits
- Eternity, God
simply gloss
the loss of enthusiasm
as the years pass,
and I feign composure when everything's crap.

**Beggar**

A beggar on the street
I pestered folk.
I pestered in Leeds
I pestered in York,
Parliament Street
and Lord Mayor's Walk,
Grosvenor, Sycamore,
until a great aunt
left shares to invest
then I pestered no more

but deep in old England pestering anew
but not on the street
at home on the phone
at meal time, prime time,
and the passage knee deep
in credit card pesterings
glossy and gold.

Embarrassed I remember
how tattered I begged
tattered and crude
when I could have learnt pestering at its best
- refined, polite
in Lloyd's, Nat West.

**Growing Old Gracefully**

The arches have fallen under my feet,
will the edifice follow? Names I forget
like my sister in law's name, er... the one with the hair net
and faces too - only last week I met this man in Parliament Street
and we talked and talked of years ago
our memories somehow out of step
when suddenly a light switched on inside my head,
before this day we'd never met.

Sometimes I put my glasses down.
It takes a morning's safari to hunt them down
and my logic's gone
my sense of smell
'Rose,' I guess as I sniff a lady's wrist,
I'm always wrong.

I rarely co-ordinate mouth and thought
- dreams and reality coalesce -
and I invite somehow
gratuitous smiles of the opposite sex
on the street, in M & S.
I suppose they think I'm harmless now
though faintly still the embers glow,
and from the years old friends avow
'you haven't changed a bit you know,'
my hair in full retreat.
On security screens I see myself - an all round view.
Transfixed, I stare.

And it's strange how cliches come full circle
- words I vowed I'd never say
like 'things were different when I was young,'
but I hear them now in conversations with my son
and fear one day I'll mouth old maxims on grace and age.
I think I'd rather rant and rage.

**In Memory of Terry**

A glut of mayflies in the sorrel
and once a tiger moth
this far north,
snow - lost in it
quail - skitterings
cold freshness,
flakes.

Then he lagged behind.
Needles of frost. Mists
and he climbed the wall, breathing white.
I missed him on the way to school.
Drifts - the deepest since '36.
Down the lane we spoke with hands, made faces.
He pressed his nose to the window pane
and acted daft.

Then daftness stopped.

I ran down to the Ings
where we lay on our backs
and all around us bleeping bats.
Owls. Lapwings.
The swish of snow.

**Ken**

Sixty years on and still surfacing
- cartwheeling down the street,
chatter - sparrows in the eaves.

The mid-summer heat.
A little boat greened.
A moorhen paddling into the reeds.

The coolness of water on our skin,
entanglements of weeds
and the swirl of fear
and I willed him to surface

- surfacing still:
skylarks, moths, long shadows,
and us hiding from whatever it was
beneath the willows.

**Rabbit**

I twitch my nose
and in the shadow of a crow
lie flat
and from what I know of fox and dog
I know there is no rabbit God
and make the most of blackness, shadows
hide beneath the sweeping willows
and prick my ears
and pick up talk
of gas and guns
and thoughts like hounds
drive me to ground
in the darkness of my head.

**Library**

The smell of burnt paper.
She leads me to the lamp with the green shade
on the charred table,

chairs still blazing
and we walk through embers to flaming shelves

anthologies smouldering
spinal blues
sienna
black
flaking off,

rare editions,
what's still to be written:

I turn the pages,

my fingers glow.

**My Stubbornness**

He stands his ground
on the lawn and in the house
never considers what's false or true
and I can't uproot his point of view
by common sense
rationale or precedence
- stickler sticks to what he thinks
his idée fixe, intransigence
- rule obsessed
opinionated dunderhead
kicks like a mule
when I lock him in the garden shed.

**Pheidippides**

Whatever history says, I run
from the dread and blood of Marathon,
the festering sun
and multitudes of nameless men
crowding in the underworld.

I cross the ridge of Pindus, south
- nightjar, owl -
and hear the words of Clemonodes
words that seeded in my head:
how by chance some are Greeks, some Persians
clinched in fears
clinched in myths
like ice that melts, ice age slow
- factions, philosophies
and yesterday's values, yesterday's snow.

Uphill the Lodos blows
and I quench my mouth with thoughts of water
resting in the cool of night
- wild olive, thyme -
darkness swallowing Attica,
and oh that darkness could black out
the blood and glare of Marathon
like that fabulous night
when three of us sleeping on pillows of rock
suddenly awoke in a sleepless dream
Diana the huntress high in the sky
and there before us on the crags
bread, water
and a note in Persian:
Festival of Light,
drink, eat,

and this the image that warms me in the mountain air,
clouds of morning reddening
- the Acropolis, the Parthenon
smell of wood smoke over Athens

egrets flying to the fields
and by my side villagers running
some faster than I
ahead with the news.

Athena, Zeus
and me honoured and feted
and on my brow a laurel wreath,
and in my head the hack and gash
vulture flap,
eyes staring dead at swooping crows.

Water splashes over the edge.
In go the dinner plates, saucers, spoons.
Mundane! I usually think of something else
as I wash up, but today:
the movements in this bowl
- swirl of water, drip and sud.

*

Can forms be repeated bowl after bowl?
- assuming my hands stay the same
since the skin's always growing, the nails
and with age, a bony change.

*

Repeating is in the shifting of things
tomorrow's sea and winds
shingle, sand
and you rushing ahead
then quiet in pools
my hand on your shoulder,
the tide flooding in.

**For M**

Together we watched the winter birds
small birds at the nuts
I hung from the branch.
Beaks slender
black throat, cap
cheeks white.
Acrobats
- blues,
pinkish
- long-tailed tits.
The quick flit.
The startled light,
anxious leaves
cold sleet and ice
and some in the sorrel
the Yorkshire mist
and what she loved most
- upside-down
primrose, green
in the black wind.

**Junkie**

Scared at first
but now it's nowt.
You've got to get it right.
In the groin.
In the arm
and the stuff must be right
or you're fucked up all night.
Right and it floods the brain and then you're floating.

Nowt to eat
mould on the bread
- syringes, fag ends
blood on the bed
keeping ahead.
Topping up.
Enough for tonight,
stuff for tomorrow.
Always a risk
pigs on your back
drought - no crack,
kicks: ketamine, hash
vomiting, cramps
and you gag for a fix.

**For S**

Sometimes you asked me to look through your bag
- a secret world of lipstick and memory.

Your mirror ageing slightly at the edges, I glimpsed myself
- that summer entrance to a stately home
a day still young with the tickets you kept.
A hotel bill,
recounting somehow the heather time,
a cockle shell
and the sound of waves on the long beach.

I peered in the corners
and a faint mist of powder
rose like nostalgia.

I smell it everywhere.

(For Audrey and Paul)

I'm always ahead of myself
looking out to sea,
something to hold on to where I am
- sunsets, horizons
though nothing's still
- the mind, the heart
and sand dissolving where I stand,
shells awash in the watery light
now red, now blue
oystercatchers in the wind
sift of shingle,
seaweed streaming like love somehow,
this way, that.

**for Mr L who talked about going back**
(For Kay and John)

the door boarded
we enter through a window
beneath the barbed wire
light the candles
and fetch the shadows
fold them into chairs, tables, the piano
madam blavatsky and the old songs
dabonavitch markova
and the arch of her back
the kazaks
the ring growing slack on your mother's finger
the bells of azinak
the stealth of snow
and frost translating stones
and shells
jackal fox
the wide-eyed owl
the eye of the solstice
closed for days
then blinking open
fire and ice
the shivering sun
wolf howl stars
and the glittering night
and where did the sky end
and the hills begin
lost cubs and weddings
bleakness and the long wind
a violin

white nights
white years

flickerings
blackness and the long way back
we strike a match
a newspaper tells us
which language we're in
which war

**Intruder**

There's an intruder in my poem
slipping down the cadence of a line.
He must have entered by the poem's back door,
or did the neighbours set me up?
Could the poem be wired?

He smokes Virginia,
words reek of it
and like a simile sometimes
he touches the hairs on the back of my neck
and calls my name.
I'm threatened by imagery and wary of rhyme
and where he hides I never know
- in the stanza facing south
the corridors between the lines,
the literal, the metaphor.

I could, of course, destroy the poem
but it's not insured
or write another and keep him out,
but he'd soon be back
in step with rhythm, metre.

Anyway, I can't pretend he isn't there,
write fiction, fantasy.

**Do-it-All**

I keep a Do-it-All under the stairs
and fetch him out every day.
He screws things up
plasters, paints
lifts the corner of my depression.

He works well at heights - chimney stacks
and when I'm manic he lowers me down
step by step.
He's very patient, practical
and tackles anything out of joint
- these floorboards, this door,
relationships,

and whatever's redundant he topples down
chimneys, rhetoric,
strips varnish, paint
down to the pine,
what's papered over - cracks and stains
- gloss, facades,
whatever pretends to be what it's not.

**Shearwaters off Istanbul**
(For Carol and Paul)

*In Greek mythology, shearwaters are the souls of the dead in perpetual flight.*

First with a glimpse of waves and wings
as if they were part of the sea itself
taking shape and riding the air -
I've followed these birds from day to day
over the waves of the Lodos winds
- souls of the dead in perpetual flight -
I watch them for their grace and skill
skimming the sea, but more than this:
the curious fear they'll settle in droves across the bay
destroying the myth behind the bird
as darkness folds their wings in night.

**House**

Meeting at angles like these nothing closes.
Winds find gaps,
my moods are rarely flush with yours
and taps they drip the night away.

On the landing floorboards creak
and doors abandon geometry.
Out of the flue woodsmoke blows
nothing flows - water, words.
As for the pipes, they clank all day,

so if we stay, it's all repairs
- plumb line sheer,
the alignment of windows, doors and joists
a joinery muting our presence here.

**Aftermath**

It lingers still,
and for solace I gorge myself on Whisky marmalade
straight from the jar
- spoonfuls of it, my mind a mess.
There's a blob on the tablecloth
the floor,
my trousers even
my hand, gummed to the jar,
I must have touched my nose, my hair,
my glasses a blur
- everywhere stickiness.

I lick the spoon, my fingers
lips
- tangy it lingers.

**Joiner**
(For Mick)

Seasoned in sun and rain,
he'd stare at the wood
as if he could see what was hidden there
its size and shape
- tables, stools
beds for newly weds, cots
pews, the bar at The Crown
- on the shelves
forgotten things - some half finished
breadboards, bats
hutches for rabbits
and raftered for years
his coffin bespoke
snugly shaped
and made to last till Judgement Day,
and the Art of the man survived his passing
- the five barred gate on Jackson's farm
fives and threes waxed and polished
an altar in alder at St. James'
- a hickory cross,
and for the methodists, one in oak,
skittles, castor cups and wooden knobs and stumps for cricket,
a mountain of sawdust for gerbils, mice,
and arms outstretched
his kitchen chair,
just fitting my back.

**Wagtails**

Their long tails flicking,
we try to get closer
before they fly off
through the cold copse,
willows trailing ice
skitterings in half light,
mists,

and it takes years edging closer
closing gaps
- a step forward then back -
pied and slender, swerve and dash
black caps bobbing round our feet,
huddling closer in the white wind.

**The Lane**

I went back and squatted on the grey cobbles
shaped like number eights
- hard and flinty like my father's speech:
'Na then, what's up lad,
swallowed thi tongue?' Drizzle
and snow that never made it
always off-white,
roofs heavy as lead.
Ducketts turning in a flash of rain
and the ancient cement,
bricks whitening, grit
loose stones,
and scraping closed the backyard door
- 'Put wood int'oil, it'll bang all night'.

The birds of the lane
- birds that never left
starlings, sparrows and the smoky crow
and everything in season coming back
vetch, chickweed in cracks
and I picked it for my mother and aunty May,
whooping cough, fevers lying low
then the ambush - thrush, measles
facts far from what I learned at school
- aphids on the underleaves
brilliant chatter
- brittle linguistics, honest vowels
sighs, glances
who drank with whom, loved,
Nellie Martin, nobbut a lass, her belly growing,
the greyness, the rain
and how important the unimportant became
my conker 94 years old,
the Spivey's cat.
Tin baths,
the rattling panes in the booming wind
- red leaves from streets away

and once a tortoise - the Dandy, the Beano
blown in the wind,
the smell of snow
cocoa
and the flood of white women coming home
and my father mumbling about the Hun:
'We'll fight the bastards on the Ings
and down the lane'
and we willed our bombs on German lanes
and hated folk we never knew.

The smell of Domestos
a thousand starlings
- a thousand things that made the lane,
swarms of wasps
greenfly dormant since last Spring
and every day a new conflation of chance and things.
Paint. Flecks.
Darkness - snecks, boots
hobnailed, steel-tipped
and you could tell who was coming down the lane,
me and my sister used to guess
- Mr. Wake, Mr. White,
voices in the mists
stammers, lisps
the jagged language of the lane.
The frantic sparrow in the window pane.
The fear in a mouse.
Window boxes
forget-me-nots,
the frenzied dog shredding the night.
And could it have been otherwise?
- the vastness of chance:
born in the next street
India, France.
Mr. White's coffin
and did he fit in
comfy, relaxed,
and all of us specialists
in acting daft, explorers

- crossing the Scarborough line
in hooded night,
sparkling minds
flattening halfpennies to pennies
on the shuddering tracks,
caterwauls, bats
stars and the Moon's eclipse
the glow of woodbines
and the sweepings of what was left behind
- Mr. Wake's betting slip
an address,
shrill swifts and the owl coming out
and scandal starting anywhere
and finding its way to the end of the lane.
The stones' decay.
Greyness, rain
and folk moving in
and weighing them up
men leaning on bikes,
frizzy permed women.
Bickerings, rows
and I wondered what they meant
beneath the words,
the sounds,
and all of us loved each others lives,
gossip flooding down the lane.

I squatted on the cobbles - moments spilling:
forests of moss on eye-level walls
glistening in rain
- the blurring, the fading
and my father quiet
- in his head words I'd heard him say aloud:
'What's it all about lad?' Then,
'Don't get above thi sen.'
'Trust no one, nowt.'
I counted the cobbles to the end of the lane.
Still the same.
It was as if I'd never left.

**Stag**
(For Kate Davies)

Driving alone at night
thoughts like flakes floating:
where I've come from
and where I'm going
patches of green, snow
an owl gliding.
How quickly things change
- seasons, moths
flies on the windscreen
and suddenly leaping
- the dazzle, the swerve
thump and judder
on the bonnet a stag
russet red
cud in his mouth
white wisp of breath.

In his wild dark eyes
shifting clouds
stealth of shadows,
myself.

**Arrest**
(For the poet Nazim Hikmet who was under threat most of his life for what he wrote and what he read.)

A smallholding in the dry hills.
His threadbare horse
chickens scrawny
and they rummaged the house
for whatever might be inside his head
in prose or poems
- under the straw,
the shimmering air.

Across the fields, bracken, poppies
cumulo nimbus over the hills
and they made little soundings in random places
thirsty drops darkening the earth
bouncing off helmets,
jeeps
then the slosh and sluice
rivulets, runnels
and the stream alive in the rush of water
and Hikmet listening
name after name flooding back
Neruda, Lorca
Macchu Picchu
gypsy songs
and in the storm
the sounds of hoofs
'Horses' 'Horses'
Hikmet's horses
the dry earth gulping,
wolf spiders, ants
riding the waters
iambics
sodden and sounding
across the hills.

Telephony, detectors
and the gendarmes came
- squelch of boots
but guests of God all the same
urgency softening in candlelight talk
till morning glistened,

then lists, lists
arid procedures
mother's maiden name
village, brothers, sisters
and from the outhouse scraps of poems
- Mayakovsky, Ahkmatova
Hikmet's lyrics.

Over the hills
cumulo nimbus shadowing.

## The Years

Searing ambition
the thunder of fear
and the terrible history of the years
the terrible history of desire
and I blurt out things of things revered
of Popes and Kings
and dare to say
there must be something else to say
but words won't bend to what I mean
- the lack of rhyme, the dearth of passion
and the swollen loneliness of mankind
in spite of what the poet might say
of islands and men
- the ferry connects this side to that
pays a cursory call and then comes back.
The endless chatter on the phone
- did you back the favourite in the 2 o'clock?
and will the tulips last till june?
And what I wrote,
decisions made not worth a mote
and whatever's left clings like ivy round the house
- belonged and belonging
images in the passing clouds.

**Eyes**

About eyes, one thing I've learned - they give you away.
My wife knew all the signs:
the vacant deceit of pretending to listen, the shifty fib,
the lack of rhyme between word and eye
and the pretence of not seeing - 'oh I didn't notice love.'
The sudden fascination with ceiling, carpet
and the spurious innocence in the meeting of eyes.

Eyes they've always betrayed me
spurning what I think and feel,
except that once - moistening, burning.

Whatever I love
is part of something else
stars : blackness,
singers, musicians on Friday nights:
real ale, Guinness.
The blackbird,
head on one side
- greenness - spring
and the tick of your bike
and the strange feeling
at the way you get on it.
Tousled in bleakness
the Shetland pony,
daffodils in snow
Moscow
and you taking photographs
of planes on the airfield.
Speechless, I watched.
Chesterfield,
my fib and you catching me out
and your rebuke
'straight as the spire,'
your voice in the darkness.
The fire in your eyes.

**Our Hens**

Kids - we talk to them
play games with them
and give them names.
Maggie, old Joe, the cock
and they hunch and squawk
peck the raw neck of the Rhode Island Red
and from the shed a cackling erupts
infects the rest
necks erect, all high on sound.

Then they settle again
- moulting moans and half-closed eyes.
A couple flare up in a scuffle of feathers.
On the sad soured land
they mimic a scratch,
dip their beaks and drink with grace.

We bury them at the garden's end
dates names
Wendy, James...

**Key**

I slammed the door
and walked round the park
blooms incongruous - drizzle
and I turned everything over
- the key in my pocket
over and over,

then crossing the line between staying and leaving
a flash of reversal
as if the decision to go were the act of going
and release enough

returning
a click of relief as I turn the key
and enter the darkness
- the gritty imaginings of 'glad he's gone'
now a listening for the lock turning.

**Onions**

We argue over anything:
- peeling onions for instance
seven or eight for a stew
and she peels off just two or three layers
but me the strangest need to peel and peel
layer after layer
and the layer after that
uncovering whiteness
and the grain of the flesh
down to the heart
till nothing's left
and all around layer upon layer
and her just standing there
eyes swimming in tears.

**bookmite**

startled scurries
panics in circles
words rushing by
footnotes addenda
oblivious to meaning
logic of print
stanzas stark prose
philosophy rhyme
hides sometimes
in a film of air between the pages
deep in the spine
morocco vellum
in the loop of an o
and where he feels safe
in bold italics
gothic roman
the closed book of night

and settles sometimes
in the silence of margins
words snowed in

**My Mistakes**

I foster mistakes
broods of them
and every day there's more of them
each with its pedigree:
investments, grammar, relationships,
and what I like best
blessed and simple
they're never contrived
never hide
never pretend to be what they're not
always close
at work at home
in the garden, the garden shed,
sleepless at night
they chatter in groups around my bed.

**Potatoes**

Each seed a foot apart
for next June's potatoes.
I entrust them to the brooding dark.

On each furrow a thistle, goose grass grows,
then the first leaf
- its curious unfolding into the world.

Late May, olive greenness crowding the furrows
and I cautiously sink my fork and lift
- a brood of them scattering
and some running back into the blackness
- pearls from the string -
whiteish, waxen,
blind in the dazzling sun.

**Dante - Addendum**

Half way through my life
I awoke in a dark wood
and started to climb the path of deliverance
when a shade appeared - Virgil, my guide,
to lead me upwards to the good,
but before the good I had to see the other side:

above a searing sea of larva
clinging to rocks, black and smouldering,
shades from the Orient, England, France
Kings and Popes,
who in the name of race, religion,
kept a burning hate alive.

Then a shade appeared beneath a crag
- Plutus, the God of wealth
and at his feet shades in thousands
and one I recognised
Calvanti of the Florentine School
who transposed freedom to free to exploit,
a practice that spread from Rome to Naples and beyond
wherefrom these shades: arms for legs and vice versa
penis nosed,
floundered in the lower Hell.
Their mouths were full of excrement.

Then sucked to husks
by leeches of the putrid fens
money lenders, bankers - Masrachio of the Roman Bourse
the Siennese Francesco,

and beyond the Styx
shades parched and scouring the deserts of Hell
clashed for dew in the morning air
making the most of bodily fluid
- these Tuscan lords, their nature arid.

And there were shades like mules harnessed to beams.
Round and round they ground the corn,
no water, rest.
These gifted shades of Genoa, Rome,
this *bolgia* bound
for neglect of shades less ably endowed.

And by the banks of the Acheron
great pagans, among them Socrates, in limbo
who questioned the shades assembled there
why some have much and many nothing
and all of them muttered
investments, profits,
speculation, peculation,
actuarial calculations
and not one uttered effort and toil
for the sin unforgiveable of lying in Hell.

And across the firey Phlegethon
shades from the richest cities of the north
who stuffed their ears to blistering needs
of natives of the Seven Seas.
Eternally condemned to famine, drought
with bulging eyes and limbs like sticks
while spheres away in the globe of Hell
bloated demons voiced the refrain
*distance absolves indifference somehow*.

Then in a cave Asconti of the Cardinal Red
- his belly rumbled,
never a bite since he came to Hell.
Surrounded by a horde of demons
- one of them donned a blood red cape
and sermonised as Asconti did
on feeding the poor whom he never fed
and so the demons one by one
showed him paintings in the renaissance style
by Giotto, Lippi
of roast venison, lamb, tagliatelli
and many more of the sumptuous dishes of Venice, Siena.
He drooled forever.

And we two poets, Virgil and I,
wandered through the plains of Hell
where nothing has meaning
save the divine design to harness punishment and crime,
power devoured by power itself
as little fish are swallowed whole
by clones voracious as themselves
and wealth swamps wealth
like vomiting mud builds layer on layer.

Then we wandered down the lanes and ginnels
the squares of Dis
static aggression in the air
- shades demented,
animal eyes in the light of despair,
eternal grief and hope abandoned.
'Oh master', I said 'so much reality, so hard to bear',
and we entered the road hidden from the souls of Hell
leading to the world above - its brightness, air.

**Shed**

So many things kept for years in the garden shed
- television, wireless smothered in dust
and still to fix her sit-up-and-beg,
cobwebs, rust
and algae spreading.

                \*

Sleepless at night I sit in the shed
- anxieties, neuroses -
the dearth of discernment in myself:
those who only cared for themselves
and those who flattered
and those who were close and should have mattered
and all the words that went unsaid.